I L♥VE Unicorns

Activity Book

Scholastic Children's Books
Euston House,
24 Eversholt Street,
London NW1 1DB, UK

A division of Scholastic Ltd
London ~ New York ~ Toronto ~ Sydney ~ Auckland
Mexico City ~ New Delhi ~ Hong Kong

Published in the UK by Scholastic Ltd, 2018

Text © Scholastic Children's Books
Illustrations © Kim Martin, represented by The Bright Agency

ISBN 978 1407 18874 4

Printed in Malaysia

2 4 6 8 10 9 7 5 3 1

Papers used by Scholastic Children's Books are made from wood
grown in sustainable forests.

www.scholastic.co.uk

Unique Unicorn

Draw lines to match the unicorns into pairs. One does not have a match – circle the unicorn that's unique!

Answers at the end of the book.

Wonderful Wings

Starting at number 1, join the dots to transform this unicorn into an alicorn!

An alicorn is a unicorn that has wings and can fly.

Castle Canter

Today's canter is to a magical kingdom! Can you spot 12 differences between the pictures?

Answers at the end of the book.

Magical Makeover

Finish doodling the hairstyles to give each unicorn a fab new look!

Add some colour to each hairstyle once you're done doodling.

Making a Splash

This unicorn is keeping cool at the waterfall! Use your stickers to add some unicorn friends to the scene.

You could even add in some butterflies and flowers!

Moonlight Match

These unicorns are meeting by the light of the moon. Colour in the picture using the colour code below to help you.

Cloud Maze

Alicorn, alicorn, fly away home! Help this young alicorn find its way through the cloud maze to join its mother.

Answers at the end of the book.

Start

Finish

Meadow Walk

Who is playing among the wild flowers?
Put the picture back in the right order to find out!
Number one has been done for you...

Word Reveal

Find all ten words in the word puzzle below – the words read forwards and down.

				D	R						K	G			
			H	R	E	S	H	I	N	E	H				
		P	R	E	O	M	E	Z	L	P	O	K			
	H	Q	X	A	X	R	W	M	N	O	R	W	R		
A	O	E	A	M	I	U	I	L	X	U	N	T	L	T	
T	O	Q	R	T	R	S	N	G	K	P	Z	N	P	A	
N	V	L	A	X	M	A	G	I	C	A	L	A	U	I	
M	E	C	R	N	L	N	S	P	N	K	R	M	C	L	
S	L	C	G	M	G	I	L	X	I	N	L	I			
	O	A	S	P	A	R	K	L	E	P	S				
	N	Z	G	O	X	M	O	Z	C						
	M	A	N	E	C	S	G								
	R	J	U	M	P	P									
	Z	L	K												
	G														

SPARKLE   MAGICAL   HOOVES

MANE   HORN

TAIL   DREAM   JUMP

WINGS   SHINE

Now unscramble the letters in green to reveal a secret word. Write the secret word here:

How to Draw a Unicorn

Follow these instructions, step by step, to create the cutest unicorn!

1

2

3

4

5

6

Draw your unicorn here:

Busy Blessing

Did you know a group of unicorns is called a 'blessing'? Count how many unicorns there are in this blessing and write the number in the box below.

Answers at the end of the book.

There are ____ unicorns.

Make a Wish!

Did you know that unicorns are such magical creatures that they have the power to grant wishes? What would you wish for? Draw or write it below.

Yummy Treats

Draw lines to give each unicorn a delicious sweet treat to eat.
The unicorn's favourite treat matches the colour of its mane.

Answers at the end of the book.

Beach Trip

On sunny days it's time to hit the beach! Create a summer scene full of unicorn friends.

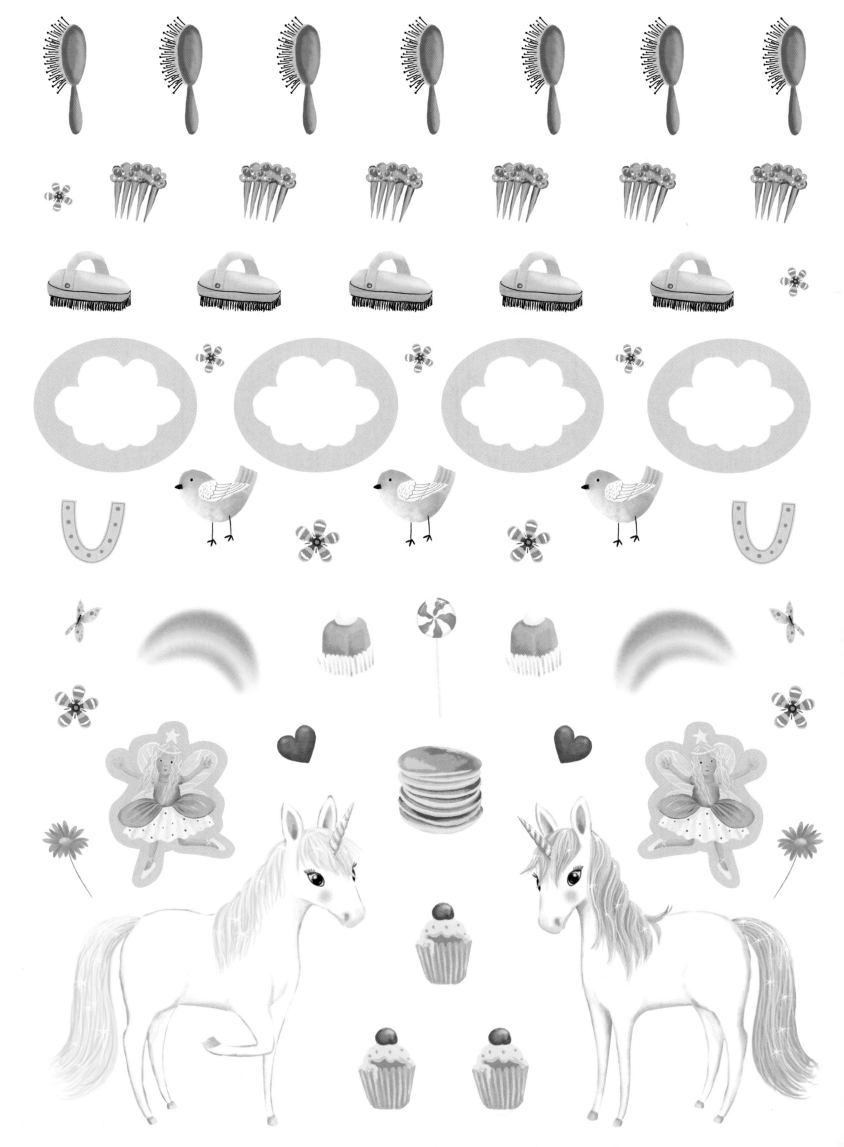

You could
even add in some
crabs, shells
and birds.

Colourful Crest

Trace over the lines to finish the picture of a fine-looking unicorn.

Add in some colour when you've finished tracing!

Legendary Friends

Which other legendary beasts are believed to have lived long ago? Read the descriptions, then unscramble the letters to reveal each mythical creature.

Place a sticker next to each creature.

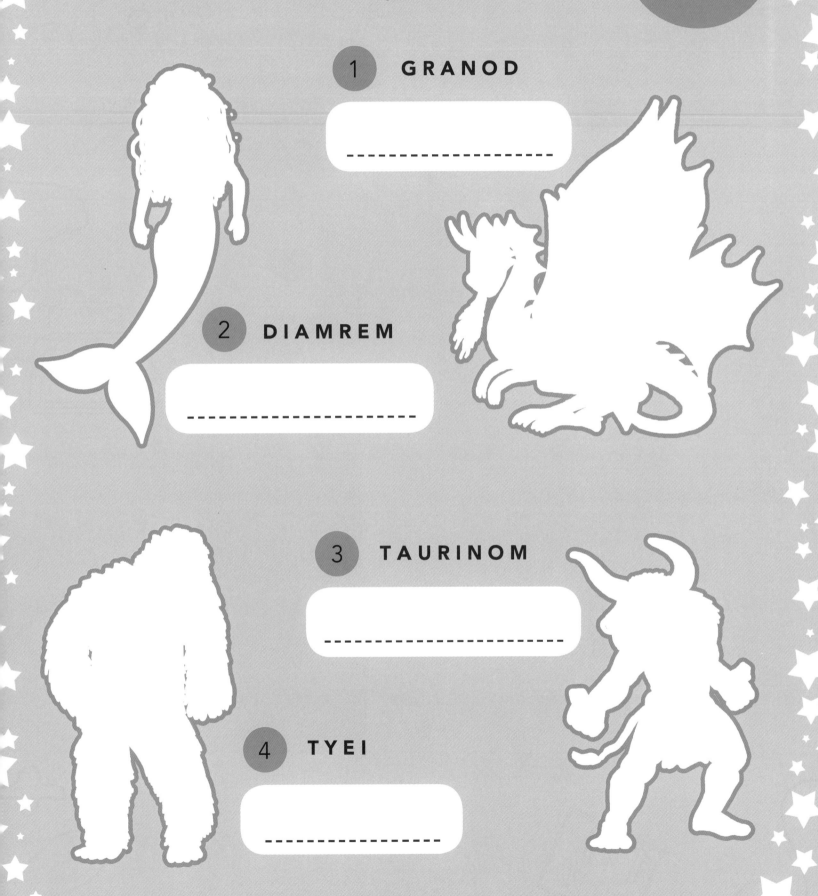

1 GRANOD

----

2 DIAMREM

----

3 TAURINOM

----

4 TYEI

Answers at the end of the book.

Pretty Postcards

Cut out the postcards on the next page, ready to send to other unicorn fans.
Then colour in the pictures below!

**Make sure
you ask an adult
to help you when
using scissors!**

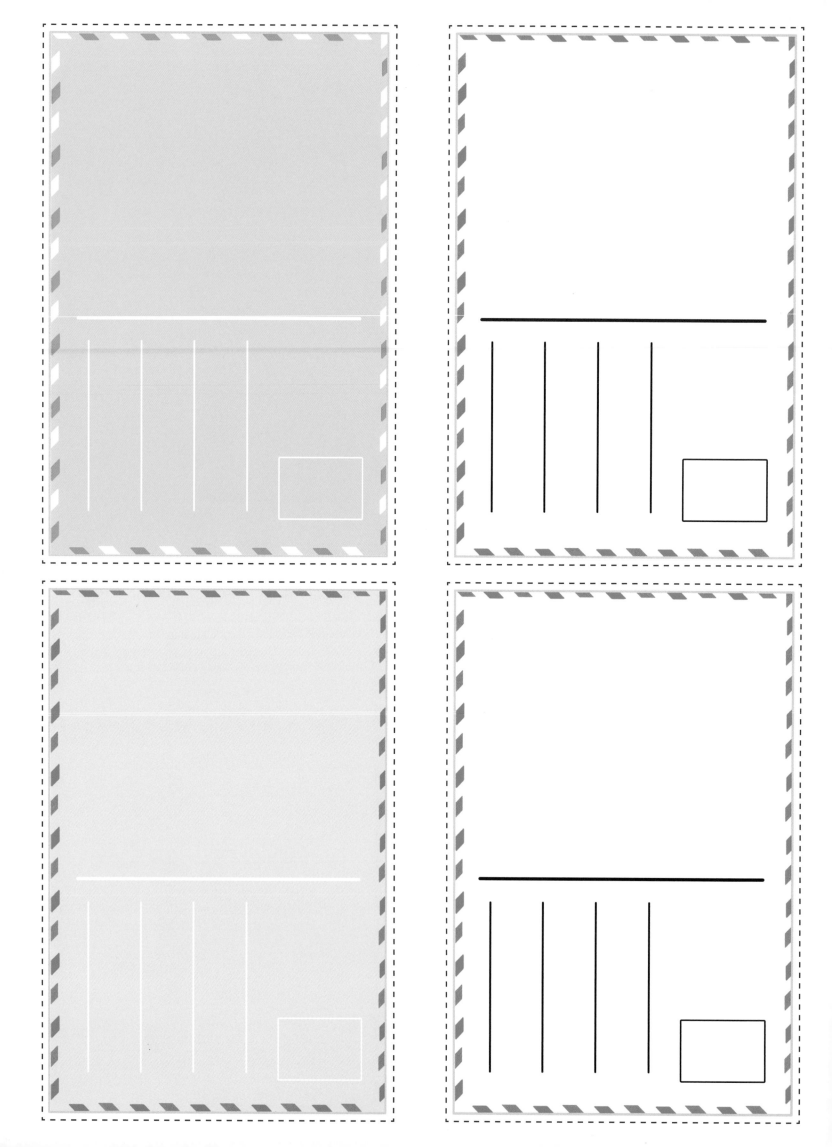

Draw a Dream

What do you think this little unicorn is dreaming of? Draw it in the bubble.

Perfect Patterns

Take a look at these picture patterns, then find the missing sticker to complete each row.

Sparkly Shadows

Unicorns come in all shapes and sizes – from dainty foals to galloping giants!
Draw lines to match each unicorn below to its shadow.

Playing in the Snow

These unicorns are having fun in the snow! Use your stickers to add more unicorn friends to the scene.

Unicorn Holiday

Rainbow Rush the unicorn is going on her travels. Choose five things to pack, then draw them in the suitcase. Add some stickers until the case is full.

What a Mess!

Princess Poppy's unicorn, Jester, has made muddy hoof prints all over the castle courtyard!
Follow the hoof prints to see where Jester is hiding.

How many hoof prints are there?

My Own Unicorn

If you had a unicorn for a pet, what would you call it? Follow the instructions to reveal a name for your very own unicorn.

First, find the month in which you were born...

January – Frosty	February – Sparkling	March – Misty
April – Dainty	May – Glittery	June – Shimmering
July – Happy	August – Starry	September – Sugary
October – Cosmic	November – Fluttering	December – Merry

And the day on which you were born...

1 – Prancer	12 – Silver Tail	23 – Floating Bubble
2 – Light Hooves	13 – Soft Socks	24 – Cupcake
3 – Leaper	14 – Bright Eyes	25 – Star Chaser
4 – Petal	15 – Candy Cloud	26 – Lovely Locks
5 – Buttercup	16 – Twilight Shine	27 – Moon Chaser
6 – Sunbeam	17 – Dazzle	28 – Chestnut
7 – Bright Swirl	18 – Sweet Face	29 – Swift Feet
8 – Ice Drop	19 – Cinnamon	30 – Firefly
9 – Daydream	20 – Phoenix	31 – Blossom
10 – Snowflake	21 – Quest	
11 – Twinkles	22 – Pearl	

Write your unicorn's name here...

Hitch a Ride

Draw yourself enjoying a magical ride on this alicorn's back, then make the picture as colourful as you can!

Answers

Unique Unicorn

Castle Canter

Cloud Maze

Meadow Walk

1 E   2 A   3 C   4 B   5 D

Word Reveal

			D	R					K	G				
		H	R	E	S	H	I	N	E		H			
	P	R	E	O	M	E	Z	L	P	O	K		
A	O	Q	X	A	X	R	W	M	N	O	R	W	R
T	O	E	A	M	I	U	I	L	X	U	N	T	L	T
N	V	Q	R	T	R	S	N	G	K	P	Z	N	P	A
M	E	L	A	X	M	A	G	I	C	A	L	A	U	I
	S	C	R	N	L	N	S	P	N	K	R	M	C	L
		L	C	G	M	G	I	L	X	I	N	L	I
	O	A	S	P	A	R	K	L	E	P	S		
		N	Z	G	O	X	M	O	Z	C			
		M	A	N	E	C	S	G					
		R	J	U	M	P							

U N I C O R N

Busy Blessing

There are **15** unicorns.

Yummy Treats

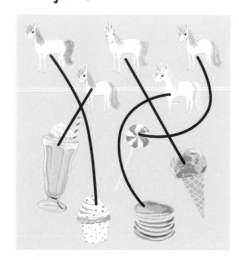

Legendary Friends

1 DRAGON

2 MERMAID

3 MINOTAUR

4 YETI

Perfect Patterns

Sparkly Shadows

What a Mess

How many hoof prints are there? **24**